D1305110

Animal World

Cows

Tessa Potter and Donna Bailey

STECK-VAUGHN
LIBRARY
A Division of Steck-Vaughn Company

The farmer on this farm
has many cows.
He keeps them for their milk.

He milks them twice a day when
their udders are full of milk.

In the summer the cows live
in a field.
They eat the grass.

But in the winter, they live
in a barn.
The farmer must feed them.

The farmer gives the cows
hay to eat.
He gives them fresh water
to drink.

The farmer keeps the barn
very clean.
He takes away the dirty straw.
He gives the cows clean, dry straw
to lie on.

Look at this cow.

She is very big.

She will soon have a calf.

8

This calf has just been born.
It lies on the grass
beside its mother.

The cow licks her new calf.
The calf is soon clean and dry.

The calf tries to stand up.
Its legs are very wobbly.
It is hungry.
It wants milk.

The cow's udder is full of milk
for her new calf.
The calf drinks her warm milk.

When a calf is five days old, the farmer
takes it away from its mother.
This girl is teaching a young calf
to drink milk from a bucket.

The calf soon learns to drink
from the bucket.
Now it does not need milk from
its mother.

14

The calf grows fast.
Here it is three weeks old.
It can eat the grass in the field.

This is another calf in the field.
The calves play together and
grow big and strong.

The calves do not drink milk now.
The farmer can have the cows' milk.
The cows eat grass, and
they make milk
for the farmer.

It is milking time.

The cows' udders are full of milk.

The cows wait for the farmer
at the gate.

18

The farmer calls the cows.
They walk in a long line
to the milking shed.
The cows want to be milked.

The cows wait outside of
the milking shed.
They go in one by one.

The first cows go into the stalls
in the shed.
The farmer gives them food.

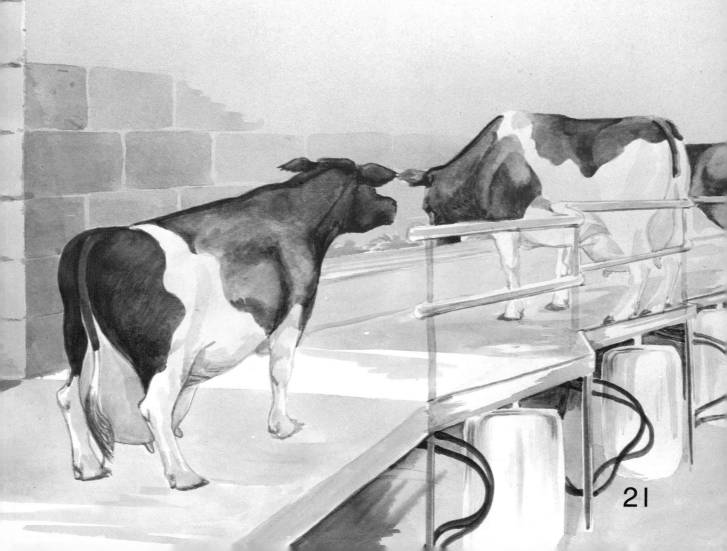

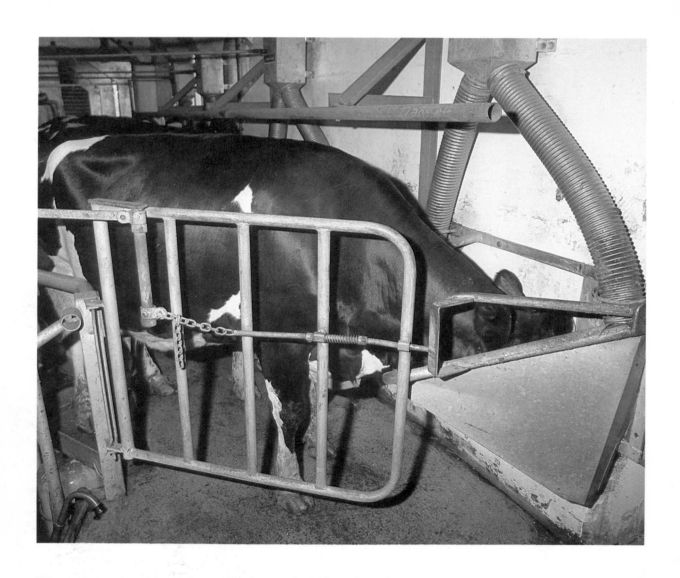

Each cow stands quietly in her stall.
She eats her food.

22

The farmer washes her udder.
No dirt must get into the milk.

The farmer has a machine
to milk his cows.

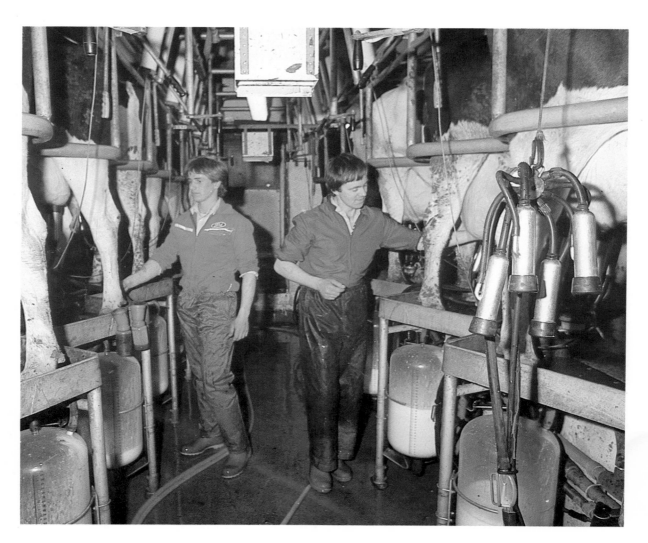

This machine sucks the milk
out of the udders.
It takes ten minutes to milk each cow.

The milk goes into jars.
There are marks on each jar so
the farmer can see how much milk
each cow has made.

When the cow has no more milk in her udder, the farmer takes off the machine.

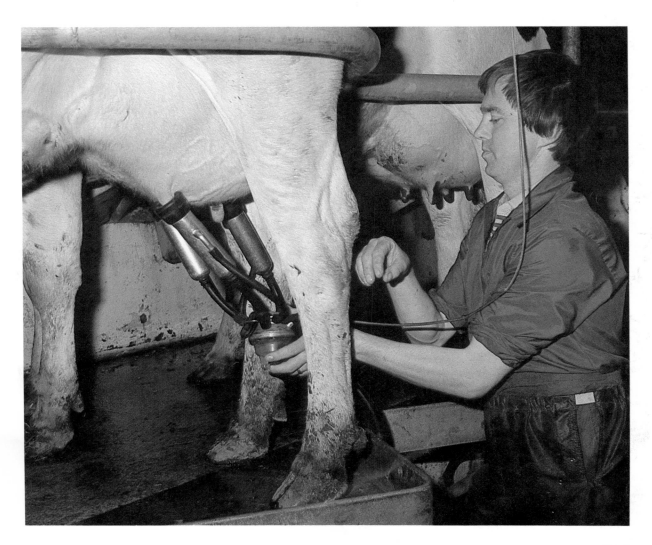

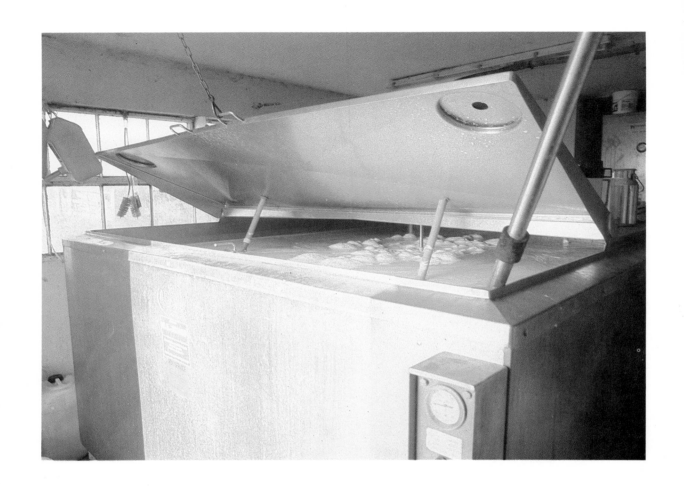

The milk from the jars is pumped
into a big tank.
The milk stays fresh and cold
in the tank.

The cows go back to their field.
Then the farmer washes the milking shed.
He keeps everything very clean.

A milk tanker comes to the farm every day.

It pumps the milk out of the tank.

It takes the milk to the dairy.

30

The milk is put into bottles and
cartons at the dairy.
Then caps are put on the bottles,
and the cartons are closed tight.

A truck takes the milk from the dairy
to the stores.
Then we buy the milk to drink.

Index

barn 5, 7

bottling 31

calf 8, 9, 10, 11, 12, 13,
    14, 15, 17

dairy 30, 31, 32

food 4, 5, 6, 11, 12, 13,
    14, 15, 16

grass 4, 15, 17

hay 6

measuring jars 26, 28

milk 2, 3, 11, 12, 13, 14, 16, 17,
    23, 25, 26, 27, 28, 30, 31, 32

milk tanker 30

milking 3, 16

milking machine 24, 25, 27

milking shed 18, 20, 21, 29

stalls 21, 22

storage tank 28, 31

straw 7

udder 3, 12, 18, 23, 25, 27

Reading Consultant: Diana Bentley
Editorial Consultant: Donna Bailey
Supervising Editor: Kathleen Fitzgibbon

Illustrated by Paula Chasty
Picture research by Suzanne Williams
Designed by Richard Garratt Design

Photographs
Cover: Bruce Coleman/Eric Crichton
Farmers Weekly: 31
Frank Lane Picture Agency: 15 (N. Elkins), 16 (Michael Clark)
Peter Greenland: 1, 4, 5, 6, 7, 8, 17, 18, 19, 22, 23, 24, 25,
    26, 27, 28, 29, 30 and 32
Eric and David Hosking: 13 and 14
NHPA: 9, 10, 11 and 12 (Joe B. Blossom)
Richard S. Orton: 32

Library of Congress Cataloging-in-Publication Data: Potter, Tessa. Cows / Tessa Potter and Donna Bailey ; [illustrated by
Paula Chasty]. p. cm. — (Animal world) SUMMARY: Discusses the lives of cows on a dairy farm. ISBN 0-8114-2626-2 1. Dai
cattle—Juvenile literature. 2. Cows—Juvenile literature. [1. Dairy cattle: 2. Cows.] I. Bailey, Donna. II. Chasty, Paula, ill. III.
Title. IV. Series: Animal world (Austin, Tex.) SF239.5.P68 1990 636.2'142—dc20 89-26080 CIP AC